This
book is
SWEET!

NATIONAL GEOGRAPHIC
KiDS

BRAiN CANDY

Seriously Sweet Facts
to Satisfy Your Curiosity

NATIONAL GEOGRAPHIC
WASHINGTON, D.C.

HAVE YOU EVER WONDERED ...

Fact-alicious!

... **WHICH IS HOTTER:** the surface of the sun or the core of the Earth?

... **HOW MANY ATOMS YOU'D HAVE TO STACK** to be as wide as one human hair?

... **WHAT COULD HAPPEN IN A BILLION SECONDS,** in a billion hours, or with a billion ... goldfish?

WELCOME TO *BRAIN CANDY*, A SWEET SELECTION OF JUICY TIDBITS, TELLING TRUTHS, UNCANNY CONNECTIONS, AND MIND-BLOWING FACTS.

Each spread in *Brain Candy* will give you a bit of information and then expand on it with related revelations. Light travels at 186,000 miles per second (300,000 km/s). At that speed, you could circle the Earth 7.5 times and get to the galaxy next door in 25,000 years! The tallest volcano in our solar system is on Mars. But just how tall is it? Three times taller than Mount Everest ... and big enough to fit the entire chain of Hawaiian Islands inside! And guess what: There are 10 quintillion insects on the planet. That's sounds like a lot, but it's hard to picture 10 quintillion of anything until you learn that it equals more than 200 million insects for every human on the planet!

LIKE LEARNING COOL FACTS AND HOW THEY'RE CONNECTED? *BRAIN CANDY* IS GOING TO BE A TREAT.

A MILLION IS A LOT.

A **MILLION** ANTS WEIGH AS MUCH AS **ONE HUMAN.**

A **MILLION** DAYS AGO THE **FIRST OLYMPICS** WERE TAKING PLACE IN **ANCIENT GREECE.**

IF YOU LIVE A **MILLION HOURS,** YOU WILL BE **114 YEARS OLD.**

A **BILLION SECONDS** IS **11,574 DAYS.**

IT WOULD TAKE A **FOOTBALL-STADIUM-SIZE BOWL** TO HOLD A **BILLION GOLDFISH.**

A **BILLION HOURS AGO,** HUMAN ANCESTORS WERE LIVING IN THE **STONE AGE.**

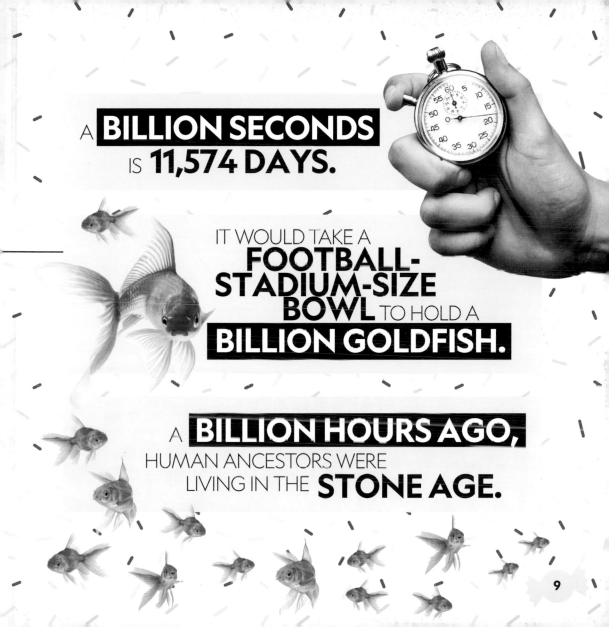

9

EVERYONE'S **TASTE BUDS** ARE DIFFERENT.

People have between **2,000** and **10,000** **taste buds.**

Some people have a **gene** that makes **cilantro** taste like **soap.**

Ageusia is the **inability to taste** anything.

Picky eaters—sometimes called **supertasters**—can have up to **twice as many** taste buds as everyone else.

11

BIRTHDAYS
are happening all the time.

MORE THAN **17 MILLION PEOPLE** AROUND THE WORLD CELEBRATE A BIRTHDAY ON ANY GIVEN DAY.

Happy **PURR-thday!**

BIRTHDAYS HAPPEN SO OFTEN THAT "HAPPY BIRTHDAY TO YOU" IS THE **MOST RECOGNIZED SONG** IN THE ENGLISH LANGUAGE.

IN A GROUP OF 23 PEOPLE, THERE'S A **50-50 CHANCE** THAT TWO OF THEM WILL SHARE THE **SAME BIRTHDAY.**

NINE OF THE TOP 10 MOST **COMMON BIRTHDAYS** IN THE UNITED STATES ARE BETWEEN **SEPTEMBER 9 AND 20.**

YOUR PET CAN GO

THE **DISTANCE.**

That's a **SWEET** ride!

14

A **LOST DOG** once **walked 2,000 miles** (3,219 km) across Australia to find its way home.

A **HAMSTER** can **run up to five miles** (8 km) a night on the wheel in its cage.

DOMESTIC CATS can **wander as far as 1.9 miles** (3 km) from home, one study found.

I was born to go FAST...

On straightaways, **NASCAR drivers** can travel **almost the length** of an **American football field** in **one second.**

NASCAR drivers experience about
3 g's of force
on every turn—the same as astronauts during a **space shuttle launch.**

NASCAR
IS ALL ABOUT
SPEED.

Pit stop crews can change four tires in **12 seconds.**

17

THE TAIL
TELLS.

Goat tails ALWAYS POINT UP.

Sheep tails **ALWAYS POINT DOWN.**

NUMBERS
CAN BE BIG—
REALLY BIG.

A **GOOGOL** IS A **1** FOLLOWED BY **100 ZEROS.**

A **GOOGOLPLEX** IS A **1** FOLLOWED BY A **GOOGOL** ZEROS.

That's 10,000,000,000,000,000,000,000,000,000,000,000,000,000,000, 000,000,000,000,000,000,000,000,000,000,000,000,000,000,000,000,000, 000,000,000,000,000.

WRITING A **GOOGOLPLEX** DOWN WOULD **TAKE LONGER** THAN THE AGE OF THE UNIVERSE.

THE LARGEST KNOWN NUMBER, GRAHAM'S NUMBER, IS **SO BIG** THAT WRITING IT DOWN WOULD BE **IMPOSSIBLE.**

THERE'S MORE THAN ONE WAY TO EAT PIZZA.

NEW YORK STYLE:
EATEN WITH YOUR
HANDS

CHICAGO DEEP-DISH:
EATEN WITH A
KNIFE AND A FORK

23

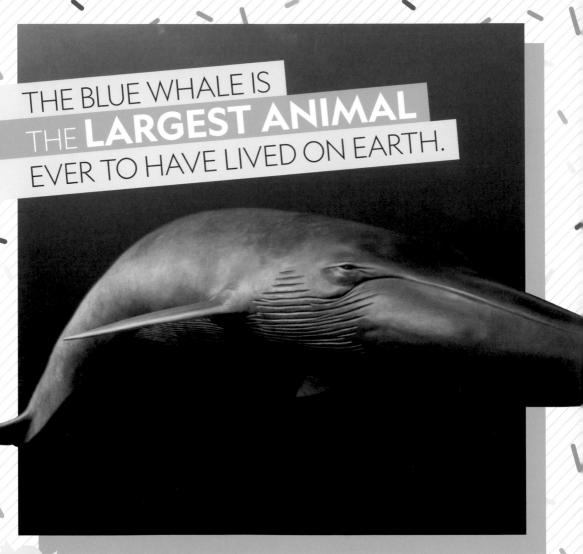

THE BLUE WHALE IS THE **LARGEST ANIMAL** EVER TO HAVE LIVED ON EARTH.

A BABY COULD **CRAWL** THROUGH A BLUE WHALE'S **BLOWHOLE.**

A TODDLER COULD **SWIM** THROUGH A BLUE WHALE'S **LARGEST VEINS.**

100 PEOPLE COULD FIT IN A BLUE **WHALE'S MOUTH.**

AFRICA IS MUCH BIGGER THAN YOU THINK.

WOW!

Africa is **LARGER THAN** China, India, Eastern Europe, and the U.S.A. combined.

Eastern Europe

China

India

AFRICA →

United States

Africa's Sahara—**THE LARGEST DESERT IN THE WORLD**—is bigger than the entire continental United States.

Although Africa is **14 TIMES LARGER** than Greenland, they often appear the same size on maps.

AFRICA

Greenland

Africa is **ALMOST TWICE THE SIZE** of Russia.

EUROPE

ASIA

ATLANTIC
OCEAN

AFRICA

INDIAN
OCEAN

SOUTH
AMERICA

ATLANTIC
OCEAN

WHY DO MAPS LIE?

Maps aren't something we question as being right or wrong. We believe that what we are looking at on paper is exactly as it would appear if we flew over it in an airplane. But maps lie—because they have to. Here's why: Earth is a sphere. A globe gives us the most accurate representation of what the world looks like, but sometimes we need to look at it flattened out—on paper. So mapmakers have a trick to solve that problem: They translate a sphere using something called projection. The most common is the Mercator projection. Created in the 16th century, it worked perfectly for measuring nautical distances, but it stretched the northern and southern poles upward, making Africa and South America appear smaller than they actually are. And here's another way maps lie: Since the first Mercator projection, maps have been generally made with north facing up—the North Pole is at the top of a world map, and Antarctica is at the bottom. But there's no scientific reason for north to be the "roof of the world." In ancient Egyptian times, the top of the world was portrayed as being in the east. Early Islamic maps positioned south at the top. What's up and what's down is really all a matter of perspective!

... Pants on FIRE!

29

EVEN THE TINIEST HAIRS ON YOUR BODY SERVE A PURPOSE.

Your **EYELASHES** **protect your eyes** from the wind.

Your **EYEBROW HAIRS** **shield your eyes** from sweat.

PEOPLE GO NUTTY FOR NOODLES.

More than **100 BILLION SERVINGS** of **instant noodles** are eaten every year worldwide.

A theater in Japan is shaped like an INSTANT NOODLES CUP.

Oh, the longest NOODLE!

The LONGEST NOODLE EVER MADE was about 2 miles (3.2 km) long.

THE **OCEAN** IS
REALLY DEEP.

HELLO?
Anybody home?

MOUNT EVEREST COULD **SIT AT THE DEEPEST POINT** IN THE OCEAN AND STILL BE **MORE THAN A MILE** (1.6 KM) **BELOW** THE SURFACE.

THE **DEEPEST PART** OF THE OCEAN— **CHALLENGER DEEP** —IS **FARTHER AWAY FROM THE SURFACE** THAN AN AIRPLANE AT **CRUISING ALTITUDE.**

THE **PRESSURE** AT THE OCEAN'S DEEPEST POINT WOULD BE COMPARABLE TO BALANCING A **2,200-POUND (1,000-KG) WEIGHT** ON **THE TIP OF YOUR FINGER.**

FOUR TIMES AS MANY PEOPLE HAVE **WALKED ON THE MOON** AS HAVE BEEN TO THE **BOTTOM OF THE OCEAN.**

This gives new meaning to "HOT DOG!"

IT'S GETTING
HOT
OUT HERE.

The temperature at the **surface of the sun** is

10,000°F

(5500°C).

Earth's core is believed to be **just as hot.**

But the **air around a lightning bolt** is **five times hotter.**

And a **supernova** is even hotter—**10,000 times hotter** than the sun.

ALCATRAZ IS AN INFAMOUS ISLAND.

California, U.S.A.'s **ALCATRAZ ISLAND** was once a prison for America's most **NOTORIOUS CRIMINALS.**

In the 1930s, Alcatraz housed infamous mobster **AL CAPONE,** who played **BANJO** in the inmate band.

NO PRISONERS were ever confirmed to have escaped from Alcatraz.

Alcatraz is rumored to be one of the **MOST HAUNTED PLACES** in the United States.

PEOPLE TAKE A LOT OF PHOTOS.

EVERY DAY, **93 MILLION** SELFIES ARE **SNAPPED.**

THAT'S **33 BILLION, 945 MILLION** SELFIES A **YEAR.**

MORE THAN **ONE TRILLION PHOTOS** ARE TAKEN **ANNUALLY.**

A DAY ON JUPITER IS
10 EARTH HOURS.

A YEAR ON JUPITER IS
12 EARTH YEARS.

43

Inventors find **INSPIRATION** in unexpected places.

SCIENTISTS MADE **LED LIGHTS** 55 PERCENT BRIGHTER AFTER THEY MIMICKED THE JAGGED SCALES ON A **FIREFLY'S LANTERN.**

THE DRAG-REDUCING **WARTY RIDGES** ON THE EDGE OF HUMPBACK WHALES' FINS INSPIRED MORE EFFICIENT **WIND TURBINES.**

A **JAPANESE BULLET TRAIN'S** STREAMLINED NOSE WAS MODELED AFTER A **KINGFISHER'S BEAK** TO MAKE IT QUIETER IN TUNNELS.

SCIENTISTS STUDIED HOW **NAMIBIAN BEETLES** COLLECT DEW ON THEIR BACKS TO MAKE **WATER COLLECTING SYSTEMS** IN DESERTS.

Where's the TUNA?

Your grocery store is all mixed up.

Strawberries, raspberries, and blackberries AREN'T REALLY BERRIES.

But bananas, eggplants, chili peppers, and oranges ARE BERRIES.

Tomatoes, bell peppers, avocados, green peas, and okra are all technically FRUITS, not vegetables.

Peanuts, almonds, pecans, and cashews aren't actually nuts; they're SEEDS.

47

THERE ARE MORE THAN

SEVEN BILLION

PEOPLE LIVING ON EARTH.

IF **EVERYONE ON THE PLANET** STOOD **SHOULDER TO SHOULDER,** WE WOULD FIT IN THE CITY OF **LOS ANGELES.**

IF **ALL THE WORLD'S PEOPLE** WERE **STACKED HEAD TO TOE**, WE WOULD REACH ABOUT **1/14** OF THE WAY TO **THE SUN.**

IF EVERYONE **LIVED AS CLOSE TOGETHER** AS PEOPLE DO IN **NEW YORK CITY,** THE WORLD'S POPULATION COULD FIT IN **NEW ZEALAND.**

IF EVERYONE **LIVED AS FAR APART** AS PEOPLE DO IN **ALASKA, U.S.A.,** WE'D NEED **108 PLANETS** TO FIT EVERYONE.

DOGS HAVE
SUPER
SENSES ...

They **smell** separately with **each nostril,** helping them figure out where **smells are coming from.**

They have **special taste buds** specifically **devoted to water.**

They can **hear sounds four times farther away** than humans can.

Their **entire bodies** are covered with **touch-sensitive nerve endings.**

Belly rubs, PLEASE!

... AND CATS HAVE SUPER SENSES, TOO.

They can **ROTATE THEIR EARS** **180** **DEGREES.**

They have **WHISKERS** **ON THEIR ELBOWS** that pick up vibrations and breezes.

They **SWEAT** from their **PAW PADS.**

They can see up to **EIGHT TIMES** **BETTER IN THE DARK** than humans can.

Roller coasters are THRILLING.

A PERSON'S **HEART RACES FASTEST** RIGHT BEFORE—NOT DURING— A **BIG DROP** ON A ROLLER COASTER.

RIDERS ON SOUTH AFRICA'S TOWER OF TERROR EXPERIENCE **TWICE THE G-FORCE** THAT ASTRONAUTS DID DURING THE **LAUNCH OF THE SPACE SHUTTLE.**

THE **FASTEST ROLLER COASTER** IN THE WORLD GOES **TWICE AS FAST** AS A CAR BARRELING DOWN A HIGHWAY.

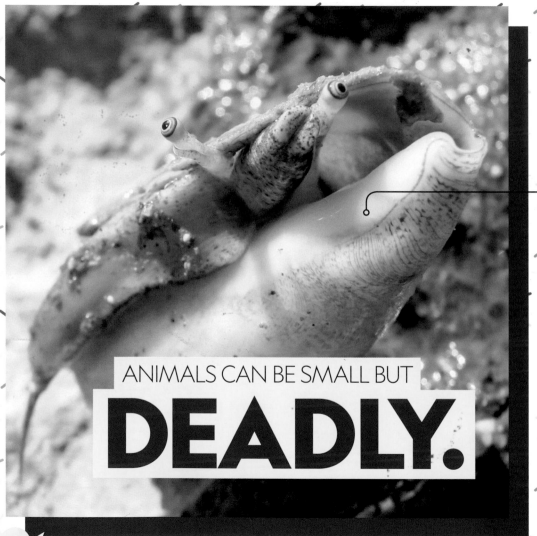

ANIMALS CAN BE SMALL BUT

DEADLY.

THE **FANGS** OF THE **SYDNEY FUNNEL-WEB SPIDER** ARE CAPABLE OF **PIERCING THROUGH FINGERNAILS.**

CONE SNAILS DELIVER **TOXIC VENOM** THROUGH A HARPOON-LIKE **TOOTH.**

BITES FROM AFRICA'S **BLOODSUCKING TSETSE FLY** CAUSE A POTENTIALLY DEADLY **SLEEPING SICKNESS.**

THE **BLUE-RINGED OCTOPUS** IS THE SIZE OF A GOLF BALL BUT PACKS ENOUGH **VENOM** TO KILL **26 PEOPLE.**

THE **HARE** REALLY SHOULD HAVE BEATEN THE **TORTOISE.**

WORLD LEADERS HAVE HAD REGULAR JOBS.

QUEEN ELIZABETH II was a **TRUCK MECHANIC** during **WORLD WAR II**.

A **FORMER DJ** became **PRESIDENT OF MADAGASCAR**.

U.S. president **BARACK OBAMA'S FIRST JOB** was scooping **ICE CREAM.**

POPE FRANCIS once worked **SECURITY** at a nightclub.

AUSTRALIA IS FAMOUS
FOR ITS BEACHES ....

You could visit **A NEW ONE** every day for more than **29** YEARS.

But before **1902** it was **ILLEGAL TO SWIM** in Australia's surf during daytime hours.

Even still, **70 PERCENT** of the country is **DESERT.**

Australia's **HYAMS BEACH** holds the world record for the **WHITEST BEACH SAND** on **EARTH.**

It would take you **37 WEEKS** to **WALK THE COASTLINE** of the Australian continent's mainland.

...AND FOR ITS
UNUSUAL ANIMALS.

KANGAROOS can **SWIM** but they can't **JUMP BACKWARD.**

The **DUCK-BILLED PLATYPUS** is one of only two mammal species that **LAY EGGS** to reproduce.

TERMITE-EATING TURTLE FROGS— one of the few frog species that **SKIP** the **TADPOLE STAGE**—look like shell-less turtles.

Inland taipan

Hi.
FRIENDSSS!

ISLAND OF DANGEROUS ANIMALS

Australia is home to lots of deadly species. This island nation—the only country that is also a continent—takes the prize for the world's most venomous snakes. Drop for drop, the eight-foot (2.5-m)-long inland taipan, also known as the fierce snake, produces the most toxic venom of any snake in the world. It may be the most venomous snake on the planet, but it's not really the most dangerous: This reclusive reptile typically keeps to itself in its remote home in southwestern Queensland and northeastern South Australia. Australia also harbors deadly spiders and sea creatures. But what's the most bizarre poisonous creature of all found only in Australia? The duck-billed platypus. Yes, this egg-laying mammal, with a bill and feet like a duck, a tail like a beaver, and fur like an otter, is actually venomous! Males of the species have spurs on their rear feet that they use to inflict a toxic blow when defending themselves against enemies or asserting themselves when competing with one another for mates. Although it would be pretty painful to be on the other end of a platypus spur, its venom is not considered dangerous to humans.

Platypus spur

Duck-billed platypus

IT TAKES A
LOT OF WORK
TO MAKE A
PROFESSIONAL
BASEBALL.

There are **108 stitches** on a **major league baseball.**

Each ball is **stitched by hand.**

Every major league baseball is **rubbed with special mud** from the Delaware River before it's used.

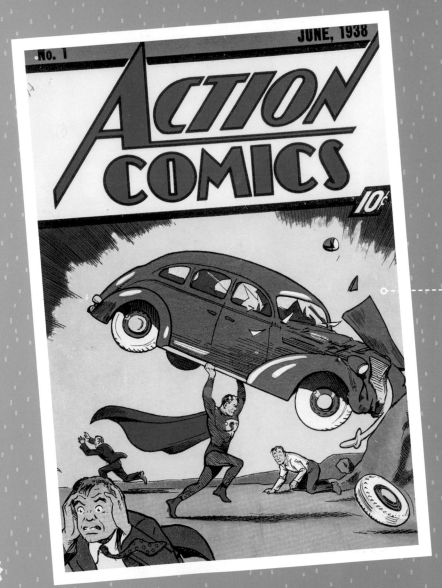

RARE COMICS ARE WORTH BIG BUCKS.

THE FIRST COMIC BOOK FEATURING SUPERMAN SOLD FOR

10 CENTS

WHEN IT WAS PUBLISHED IN 1938.

A COPY OF THAT COMIC SOLD FOR

$3.2 MILLION

AT AN AUCTION IN 2014—THE HIGHEST PRICE EVER PAID FOR A COMIC.

SOME ANIMALS GLOW IN THE DARK.

Anglerfish

VAMPIRE SQUID EJECT **BIOLUMINESCENT MUCUS** FROM THEIR ARMS TO **DEFEND THEMSELVES.**

FIREFLIES GLOW TO HELP THEM FIND A **MATE.**

You make me GLOW with joy!

MORE THAN **80 PERCENT** OF DEEP-SEA CREATURES ARE **BIOLUMINESCENT.**

Cycloseris erosa coral

SOME MILLIPEDES GLOW UNDER **BLACK LIGHT.**

Mandarin fish

73

RUBBER DUCKS
DO MORE THAN JUST FLOAT
IN THE TUB.

A five-story inflated yellow duck **TRAVELS TO CITY HARBORS** around the world.

They **STARRED ON TELEVISION** when Ernie from *Sesame Street* made the song "Rubber Duckie" a hit.

In 1992, a crate with 28,000 rubber ducks **FELL OFF A CARGO SHIP** in the North Pacific.

Scientists have been tracking them to learn about **OCEAN CURRENTS.**

FOOD
IS FOR MORE THAN JUST EATING.

I'm feeling TOASTY!

Rye bread can WIPE SMUDGES OFF WALLS.

Cold plain yogurt can relieve SUNBURN PAIN.

Banana peels can SHINE SILVER.

ANIMALS CAN HAVE UNEXPECTED RELATIVES.

HYENAS
ARE MORE CLOSELY
RELATED TO
CATS THAN TO DOGS.

ELEPHANTS' CLOSEST LIVING RELATIVES ARE
MANATEES.

A LOT CAN HAPPEN IN

ONE MINUTE.

IN SIXTY SECONDS ...

... A **HUMMINGBIRD** CAN **FLAP ITS WINGS** AROUND **4,000 TIMES.**

... **189,600 TONS** (172,000 T) OF **WATER** FLOW OVER **NIAGARA FALLS.**

... YOU WILL **BLINK 15 TO 20 TIMES.**

... THE **CURRENT WORLD CHAMPION** CAN **SOLVE A RUBIK'S CUBE** **12 TIMES.**

... THE **AVERAGE THIRD GRADER** CAN **READ** ABOUT **150 WORDS.**

Taking care of your TEETH used to be a pain.

PUCKER UP!

DURING THE MIDDLE AGES, PEOPLE THOUGHT **KISSING A DONKEY** HELPED RELIEVE A **TOOTHACHE**.

DIVERS EXPLORING A 17TH-CENTURY SHIPWRECK FOUND A **GOLDEN TOOL** THAT WAS BOTH A **TOOTHPICK** AND AN **EARWAX SPOON**.

ANCIENT EGYPTIANS USED TOOTHPASTE MADE OF **OX HOOVES** AND **BURNT EGGSHELLS**.

BRISTLES ON THE FIRST TOOTHBRUSHES WERE MADE FROM **PIG HAIR**.

SOUND TRAVELS
REALLY QUICKLY.

The speed of sound is about **767 MILES AN HOUR** (1,235 km/h).

Sound travels **FOUR TIMES FASTER** through water than through air ...

... and **TEN TIMES FASTER** through wood than through air.

85

AIRPLANES HAVE COME A LONG WAY ...

The **first flight** lasted just

12 SECONDS.

That's $\frac{1}{1,470}$ as long as a flight from **Los Angeles to New York City.**

LES → NEW YORK
16, 2017

LAX
12:00 PM

JFK
4:15 PM

FLIGHT
BC463

GATE
8A

SEAT
17B

BOARDING
11:45 AM

Again, AGAIN!

Today the **world's biggest** passenger plane, the Airbus A380, can carry up to **853 PEOPLE.**

The **first flying airplane** could hold only **one** of its two inventors.

... AND SO HAVE
COMPUTERS.

My name is WOODY!

THE **FIRST COMPUTER MOUSE** WAS **MADE OF WOOD.**

THE **FIRST PROGRAMMABLE DIGITAL COMPUTER** WEIGHED 30 TONS (27 T) AND **TOOK UP AN ENTIRE ROOM.**

TODAY'S TINIEST COMPUTER IS THE SIZE OF A **GRAIN OF RICE.**

THE REAL-LIFE
BATMAN

Click! Clicky click! Clickely-click-click-click! What's that?
You don't speak bat? You could! Scientists have found that humans can actually learn echolocation, which is the way bats and dolphins (and some other animals) make sounds and use the echoes of those sounds to navigate the world around them.

Bats use echolocation to "see" prey as they hunt at night. Humans who were born without the ability to see or who have lost their vision can use sound in the same way. A man named Daniel Kish, who lost his sight as a baby, uses fast tongue clicks—two or three per second—to get around. His nickname is the "real-life Batman," because he uses the same technique that bats use to navigate in the dark. He can uncover important details about a place using these clicks, like whether objects in a room are big or small, and made of metal or wood. Because he can "see" so well, he is able to do things—such as hiking—that would otherwise be difficult. Even people with perfect vision can learn this skill.

Daniel Kish

THE **LARGEST MOUNTAIN** ON EARTH IS A **VOLCANO** THAT'S MOSTLY **UNDERWATER.**

Hawaii's **Mauna Loa** is **56,330 FEET** (17,170 m) from **base to top,** but three-quarters of it is below the **ocean's surface.**

From its peak to its base,
Mauna Loa is

ALMOST TWICE AS TALL as
MOUNT EVEREST, the tallest
mountain on Earth above sea level.

Mauna Loa is so heavy that the
ocean floor beneath it has sunk
26,000 FEET (8,000 m).

THE TALLEST KNOWN MOUNTAIN IN OUR SOLAR SYSTEM IS A

VOLCANO ON MARS.

Olympus Mons is 16 miles (26 km) high—about **three times taller** than **Mount Everest.**

Hello my name is

Olympus Mons

Olympus Mons is about as **wide** as the **U.S. state** of **Arizona.**

The **entire chain** of **Hawaiian Islands** could **fit inside** Olympus Mons.

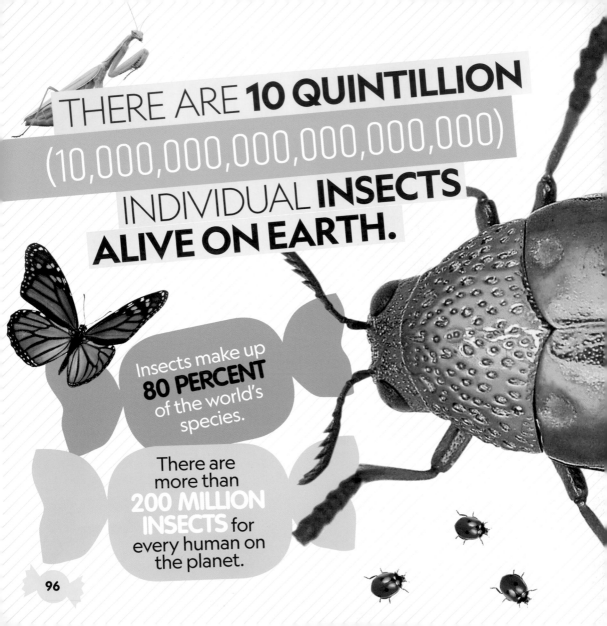

THERE ARE **10 QUINTILLION** (10,000,000,000,000,000,000) INDIVIDUAL **INSECTS ALIVE ON EARTH.**

Insects make up **80 PERCENT** of the world's species.

There are more than **200 MILLION INSECTS** for every human on the planet.

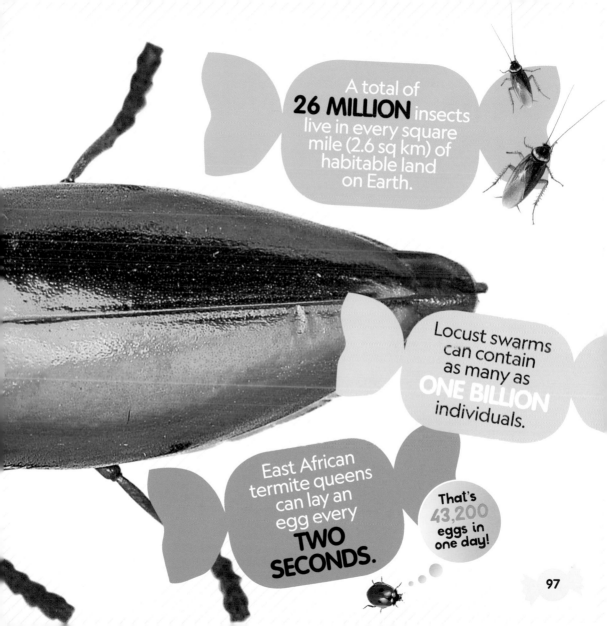

A total of **26 MILLION** insects live in every square mile (2.6 sq km) of habitable land on Earth.

Locust swarms can contain as many as **ONE BILLION** individuals.

East African termite queens can lay an egg every **TWO SECONDS.**

That's 43,200 eggs in one day!

THE STATE OF ALASKA IS
REALLY BIG...

ALASKA
IS **BIGGER**
THAN CALIFORNIA,
TEXAS, AND
MONTANA
COMBINED.

MORE THAN
HALF OF THE ENTIRE
U.S. COASTLINE
IS IN
ALASKA.

IT WOULD TAKE JUST OVER **FIVE ALASKAS** TO FIT INTO THE CONTINENTAL **UNITED STATES.**

IF ALASKA WERE A **COUNTRY,** IT WOULD BE THE **33rd LARGEST** IN THE WORLD.

HELLO? Anybody home?

... AND THE STATE OF **RHODE ISLAND** IS REALLY SMALL.

COZY!

Rhode Island is **so small** it could **fit into Alaska** **425 times.**

Greetings from RHODE ISLAND USA

The **second smallest state** (Delaware) is still **nearly twice** Rhode Island's size.

It takes only about an hour to **drive across the whole state.**

UNICORNS **ARE** REAL (SORT OF).

The **NARWHAL** is often called "**THE UNICORN OF THE SEA**" thanks to its long, pointy tooth (tusk).

People used to buy powdered "**UNICORN HORN**," believing it was an antidote to poison. (It was actually the **TOOTH OF THE NARWHAL**.)

The unicorn is the **NATIONAL ANIMAL** of Scotland.

Shaggy "**SIBERIAN UNICORNS**"—actually members of an extinct species of rhinoceros—roamed Asia 29,000 years ago.

Birds are AMAZING animals.

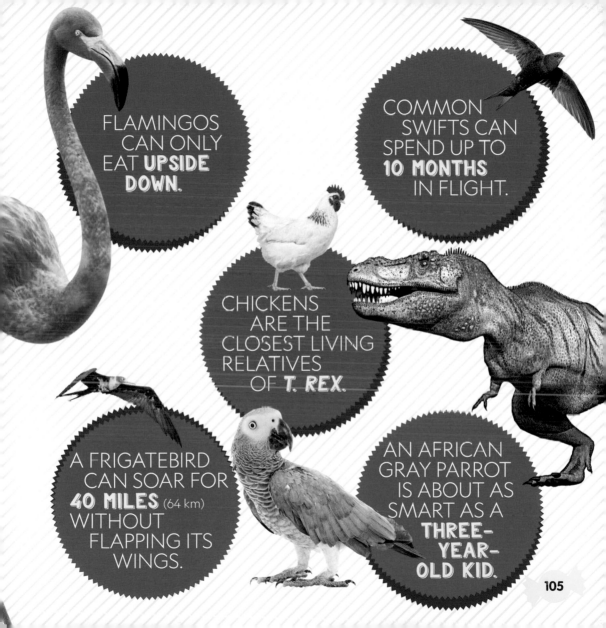

FLAMINGOS CAN ONLY EAT **UPSIDE DOWN.**

COMMON SWIFTS CAN SPEND UP TO **10 MONTHS** IN FLIGHT.

CHICKENS ARE THE CLOSEST LIVING RELATIVES OF **T. REX.**

A FRIGATEBIRD CAN SOAR FOR **40 MILES** (64 km) WITHOUT FLAPPING ITS WINGS.

AN AFRICAN GRAY PARROT IS ABOUT AS SMART AS A **THREE-YEAR-OLD KID.**

EATING
IN SPACE

ISN'T EASY.

BREAD IS BANNED ON THE INTERNATIONAL SPACE STATION BECAUSE **FLOATING CRUMBS** COULD GET IN **ASTRONAUTS' EYES.**

SOME ASTRONAUTS ADD **HOT SAUCE** TO THEIR FOOD BECAUSE **MICROGRAVITY** DULLS THEIR **SENSE OF TASTE.**

ASTRONAUTS DRINK A FILTERED MIX OF **RECYCLED SHOWER WATER, URINE, AND SWEAT.**

IN 1965, AN **AMERICAN ASTRONAUT SMUGGLED** A **CORNED-BEEF SANDWICH** ABOARD A **SPACEFLIGHT.**

HACKS

When astronauts leave Earth for the International Space Station, they leave gravity behind too. Microgravity—where gravity is very weak—makes everyday activities in the International Space Station a challenge. Imagine going to the bathroom and immediately floating right off the toilet! *Awkward.* Astronauts must put on a seat belt to stay put until they're, ahem, done. Even sleeping brings challenges. Instead of covering up with blankets, which would float away, astronauts have to crawl into sleeping bags that are attached to a wall. Even something as simple as making a sandwich is a challenge in space: Crumbs can lead to big problems on the International Space Station if they float away and get stuck in equipment. The solution? Astronauts substitute tortillas for bread. And sandwich staples like peanut butter and jelly are squeezed out of tubes to make spreading easy. Setting the table for a meal in a place where everything floats isn't typical either. Tools like scissors to open squeeze tubes are connected to a tether and attached to a wall or table, while other objects like cups and utensils stay put with the help of Velcro. Problem-solving is an important job requirement for astronauts.

THE SUN IS THE CLOSEST
STAR TO EARTH.

Going **60 MILES** an hour (96.5 km/h), it would take about **177 YEARS TO DRIVE TO THE SUN.**

EVERY STAR in the night sky is **BRIGHTER** than the **SUN,** but the sun appears to be the **BRIGHTEST** because it's so close.

The next closest stars to Earth are **ALPHA CENTAURI A AND B.** It takes about **4.3 YEARS** for **LIGHT** from these stars to reach Earth; it takes only **8 MINUTES** and **20 SECONDS** from the sun.

SHOES AND HUMANS ARE "SOLE" MATES.

People have been wearing shoes for **40,000 YEARS.**

The world's oldest leather shoe is **1,000 YEARS OLDER** than the Great Pyramids of Giza.

Shoes **CHANGED THE WAY** humans walk.

Until the 1800s, there was **NO DIFFERENCE** between a right shoe and a left shoe.

113

Don't be such a SCAREDY-CAT!

PEOPLE ARE SUPERSTITIOUS.

MORE THAN **50 PERCENT** OF AMERICANS **KNOCK ON WOOD** TO **AVOID BAD LUCK.**

IN SPAIN, PEOPLE **EAT 12 GRAPES** AT MIDNIGHT ON **NEW YEAR'S EVE** TO HAVE **GOOD LUCK** THROUGHOUT THE YEAR.

IN SOME COUNTRIES, IT'S **BAD LUCK** TO **TRIM YOUR FINGERNAILS** OR TOENAILS **AFTER DARK.**

IN SOME CULTURES, **FISH** ARE SYMBOLS OF **GOOD LUCK** AND **WEALTH.**

115

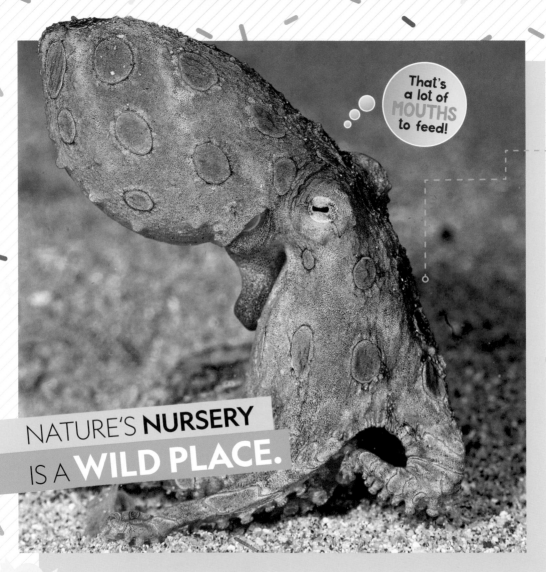

That's a lot of **MOUTHS** to feed!

NATURE'S **NURSERY** IS A **WILD PLACE.**

Some octopuses lay up to **100,000 EGGS** at a time.

Koala babies eat their mothers' poop until they're old enough to **DIGEST FOOD** on their own.

When they're born, baby elephants **WEIGH ABOUT 200 POUNDS** (91 kg).

YOUR BODY DOES **IMPORTANT THINGS—** EVEN WHEN YOU'RE NOT PAYING ATTENTION. **EVERY DAY ...**

... your **heart beats** about
100,000 times.

... you **shed** about **35,000**
dead skin cells.

... you **take** about
23,000 breaths.

... you **make 34 to 68 ounces** (1 to 2 L)
of spit.

119

Ants are PICKY.

ANTS THAT LIVE **MORE THAN 60 MILES** (100 KM) FROM THE **OCEAN PREFER SALTY** OVER SWEET FOODS.

I only eat ORGANIC.

ANTS DON'T LIKE THE **SMELL** OF **LEMON.**

SOME ANTS PREFER THE **SMELL** OF **HONEYDEW** OVER OTHER SWEET THINGS.

HUMANS ARE **STILL** EVOLVING.

WE'RE TALLER NOW than we were 150 years ago.

DUTCH PEOPLE HAVE GROWN THE MOST— about seven inches (18 cm) on average.

OUR HEADS HAVE GOTTEN BIGGER
to hold bigger brains.

Some people are now **BORN WITHOUT VESTIGIAL BODY PARTS** (things that no longer serve a purpose) like an appendix or wisdom teeth.

123

PREHISTORIC ANIMALS WERE

HUGE.

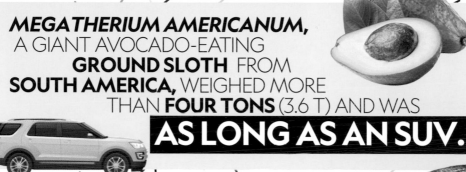

MEGATHERIUM AMERICANUM, A GIANT AVOCADO-EATING **GROUND SLOTH** FROM **SOUTH AMERICA,** WEIGHED MORE THAN **FOUR TONS** (3.6 T) AND WAS **AS LONG AS AN SUV.**

TITANOBOA, THE **LARGEST SNAKE EVER,** WAS AS **LONG AS A SCHOOL BUS** AND AS **WIDE AS A TRUCK TIRE.**

THE **WORLD'S LARGEST RODENT EVER—** APPROPRIATELY CALLED **MEGARODENT—**WAS **LARGER THAN A BISON** AND **FOUGHT OFF SABER-TOOTHED CATS** IN SOUTH AMERICA'S RAINFORESTS.

SKYSCRAPERS COME
in many sizes.

It would take more than **15** of the **WORLD'S SMALLEST SKYSCRAPER,** in Wichita Falls, Texas, U.S.A., to reach the top of the

Space Needle in Seattle, Washington, U.S.A.

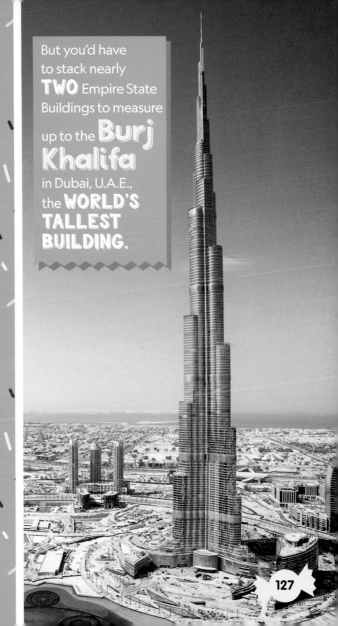

But you'd have to stack nearly **TWO** Empire State Buildings to measure up to the **Burj Khalifa** in Dubai, U.A.E., the **WORLD'S TALLEST BUILDING.**

The Space Needle is less than **HALF THE HEIGHT** of the **Empire State Building** in New York City.

THE MOON IS AN AVERAGE OF

238,855

MILES (384,399 KM) AWAY FROM EARTH.

All our **SOLAR SYSTEM'S PLANETS** could **FIT IN THE DISTANCE** between Earth and the moon.

If you **LINED UP** all of **EARTH'S BEACHES** end to end, they would **REACH THE MOON.**

It took about **THREE DAYS** for the **FIRST ASTRONAUTS** who **WALKED** on the **MOON** to get there.

If you could **WALK TO THE MOON,** it would take you **NINE YEARS.**

WORDS
ARE
WACKY.

IT'S BEEN ESTIMATED THAT A **NEW WORD IS CREATED** EVERY **98 MINUTES.**

WEBSTER'S ONCE PUBLISHED A **DICTIONARY** ACCIDENTALLY FEATURING THE **MADE-UP WORD "DORD."**

"MONTH," "PURPLE," AND **"WALRUS" DON'T RHYME** WITH ANY OTHER ENGLISH WORDS.

"SWIMS" IS STILL "SWIMS" EVEN WHEN YOU TURN IT **UPSIDE DOWN.**

¡DORD!

Ernest Vincent Wright

STAY OUT OF IT

Think about how much time it takes you to finish writing a book report. Now think about how long it would take you if you weren't allowed to use the letter e. A lot longer, probably!

In 1939, author Ernest Vincent Wright self-published a book called *Gadsby* that included 50,000 words—not one of them contained an e. No "he," "she," "the," or any other word or form of a word containing the fifth letter of the alphabet. To complete his story, Wright had to tie down the "e" button on his typewriter so that the vowel couldn't accidentally slip in. Though the book wasn't popular at the time, it's celebrated now as a major accomplishment.

A STYLE OF WRITING THAT DELIBERATELY **OMITS A LETTER** OR LETTERS IS CALLED **A LIPOGRAM.**

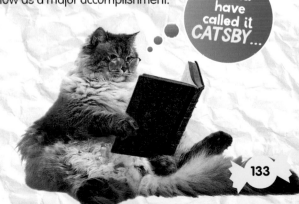

Should have called it CATSBY...

THERE ARE MORE WAYS TO CATCH A COLD THAN THE FLU.

There are only **three types** of **flu viruses,** but ...

This
BLOWS...

... more than **200 types** of viruses can cause a **common cold.**

135

FIREWORKS
HAVE BEEN
AROUND FOR A
LONG TIME.

The Chinese first created them **2,000 YEARS AGO** by throwing bamboo into a fire.

Henry the VII of England had fireworks at his wedding in **1486.**

HENRY VII
1485-1509

1ST

On America's first Fourth of July celebration, in **1777,** all the fireworks were orange.

PEOPLE **GET A KICK** OUT OF SOCCER.

Kids in a **fishing village** in **Thailand** play soccer on a **floating field.**

A former **Romanian** soccer player wore his **underwear** inside out for **good luck** on game days.

At the annual **Robocup,** hundreds of **six-inch** (15-cm)-tall **robots** from around the world face off in **soccer matches.**

SOME REPTILES CAN

FLY.

WHEN **DRACO LIZARDS LEAP THROUGH THE AIR,** SKIN BETWEEN THEIR RIBS **OPENS LIKE AN UMBRELLA.**

PTEROSAURS FLEW 78 MILLION YEARS BEFORE **BIRDS DID.**

FLYING SNAKES CAN **GLIDE** THE LENGTH OF **A SOCCER FIELD.**

PEOPLE EAT A LOT OF HOT DOGS.

HOTDOGS

Americans eat an estimated **20 BILLION** hot dogs every year.

You're the **WEINER!**

The world record for the most hot dogs eaten is **72** in **10 MINUTES.**

INVENTED IN 1484, hot dogs have been eaten since **before** the United States existed.

ENJOY OUR *Delicious* 25¢ **HotDogs** BEST IN TOWN!

143

THE ARCTIC IS SO
COLD...

... THE AVERAGE WINTER **ARCTIC TEMPERATURE** IS **MINUS 40°F** (-40°C).

... **ARCTIC FISH** MAKE THEIR OWN **"ANTIFREEZE"** TO KEEP THEIR BLOOD FROM FREEZING.

... A **VAULT BUILT** INTO A FROZEN ARCTIC MOUNTAIN CAN SAFELY STORE THE SEEDS OF MORE THAN **930,000** FOOD CROPS.

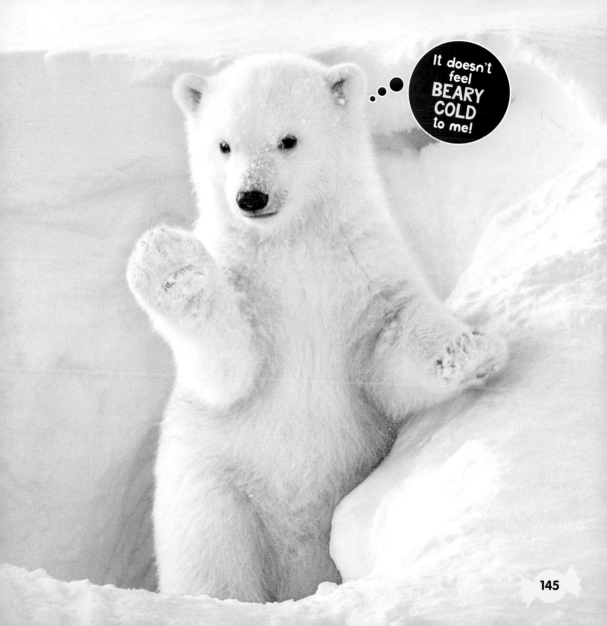

... BUT ANTARCTICA IS
COLDER.

ANTARCTICA HOLDS THE RECORD FOR **COLDEST RECORDED TEMPERATURE,** AT **MINUS 136°F** (-93°C)— THAT'S COLDER THAN **DRY ICE.**

AN ICEBERG THE SIZE OF **DELAWARE, U.S.A.,** THAT WEIGHED **1.1 TRILLION TONS** (1 TRILLION T) BROKE OFF ANTARCTICA IN 2017.

FIFTY MILLION YEARS AGO, ANTARCTICA WAS COVERED IN A **TROPICAL RAINFOREST.**

A
TROPICAL
VACATION
sounds
nice...

A British company created a **HYBRID TOMATO PLANT** that grows **tomatoes** on top and **potatoes** on the bottom.

Potatoes and tomatoes are both part of the **NIGHTSHADE FAMILY**.

Americans consume **MORE POTATOES** than any other vegetable. The second most popular vegetable? The tomato (which is technically a fruit).

PEOPLE
PRODUCE TONS OF
TRASH.

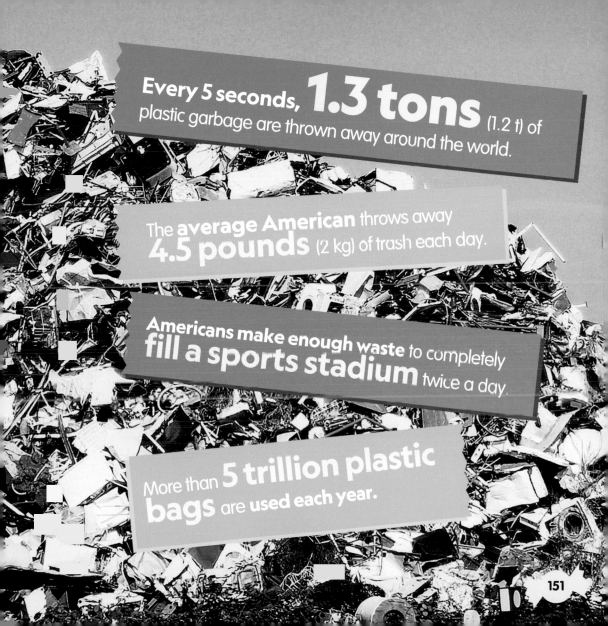

Every 5 seconds, **1.3 tons** (1.2 t) of plastic garbage are thrown away around the world.

The **average American** throws away **4.5 pounds** (2 kg) of trash each day.

Americans make enough waste to completely **fill a sports stadium** twice a day.

More than **5 trillion plastic bags** are **used each year.**

IN YOUR **LIFETIME** YOU WILL ...

... **YAWN** SOME **250,000 TIMES.**

... **EAT** MORE THAN 2,000 POUNDS (907 KG) OF **PIZZA.**

... **READ** MORE THAN **1,000 BOOKS.**

... **BRUSH YOUR TEETH** FOR ABOUT **43 DAYS.**

153

CLOUDS ARE WILD.

A TYPICAL CUMULUS CLOUD **WEIGHS** AS MUCH AS **100 ELEPHANTS.**

AT ANY GIVEN MOMENT THERE ARE **2,000 THUNDERSTORMS** OCCURRING ON EARTH.

A PYROCUMULUS CLOUD = A CUMULUS CLOUD FORMED BY THE HOT AIR FROM **WILDFIRES**

We all SCREAM for ICE CREAM.

SOME **ANCIENT ROMANS** ATE **SNOW** **SWEETENED** WITH **FRUIT** OR **HONEY.**

AT **7.5 GALLONS** (28 L) PER PERSON A YEAR, **NEW ZEALAND** CONSUMES THE **MOST ICE CREAM** OF ANY COUNTRY.

CHINESE EMPERORS LIVING OVER **1,000 YEARS AGO** MADE WHAT MAY HAVE BEEN THE **FIRST DAIRY ICE CREAM** FROM COW, GOAT, AND BUFFALO MILK.

Literally!

SPIDERS EAT A TON OF FOOD.

On average, **a spider eats 2,000 insects** annually.

Spiders collectively eat as much as **882 million tons** (800 million t) of **prey** every year.

The **weight of insects** annually consumed by spiders is about the same as the **combined weight of all humans** living on Earth.

159

YOUR **FAVORITE DUOS** DIDN'T ALWAYS GO HAND IN HAND.

THE **POP-UP TOASTER** WAS INVENTED IN **1919**, BUT **PRE-SLICED** BREAD WASN'T SOLD UNTIL **1928**.

PEANUT BUTTER WAS INVENTED IN THE **1880s**, BUT THE JELLY WE USE IN OUR **PB&J** SANDWICHES WASN'T INVENTED UNTIL **1917**.

YOU COULD **WATCH A TV IN 1927** BUT YOU COULDN'T USE **A REMOTE** TO TURN IT ON UNTIL **1950**.

THE **SPEED** OF LIGHT IS **186,000** miles per second (300,000 km/s). At that speed, **you could ...**

Earth

... circle Earth
7.5 times in one second.

Andromeda

... get to the galaxy **next door**
in **25,000** years.

GN-Z11

... reach the farthest galaxy **(that we
know of)** in **13.4 billion years.**

CHEETAHS CAN RUN UP TO 60 MILES AN HOUR (96.5 KM/H).

That's almost THREE TIMES as fast as the WORLD'S FASTEST HUMAN ...

... and only **HALF** as fast as a **SKYDIVER.**

A cheetah can **REACH FULL SPEED** in just **THREE SECONDS.**

165

CHAMELEONS HAVE SOME OF THE FASTEST TONGUES ON EARTH.

THE ROSETTE-NOSED CHAMELEON CAN SHOOT OUT ITS TONGUE AT A SPEED OF ABOUT **8,500 FEET** PER SECOND (2,600 M PER SECOND).

THAT'S AN ACCELERATION OF UP TO **264 TIMES** THE FORCE OF GRAVITY.

THAT'S **88 TIMES** AS FAST AS THE **ACCELERATION** OF NASA'S SPACE SHUTTLE PROPELLING INTO **ORBIT.**

167

AMAZING ANIMAL
TONGUES

Like us, animals use their tongues to eat and drink—and occasionally to clown for the camera. But some animals have superweird tongues that go above and beyond the basics.

Chameleons' tongues are not only fast; they're also mind-bogglingly long—up to one and a half times their body length! A sticky mucus 400 times thicker than human saliva sits on the end of these extended appendages, helping the lizards snag and reel in their unsuspecting insect prey.

Sun bears roll out their 10-inch (25-cm)-long tongues to dig out treats from tight spots—especially the yummy bugs that scurry under logs in the forests of southern China where they live. Anteaters can consume up to 30,000 ants and termites every day with their two-foot (0.6-m)-long, spaghetti-shaped tongues, which are covered in a sticky saliva perfect for capturing insects.

Some animals use their tongues to deceive their predators or their prey. The alligator snapping turtle—the largest freshwater turtle in North America—has a piece of red flesh at the end of its tongue that looks like a worm. When curious frogs and fish passing by move in to investigate, the ready reptile snatches them up. Talk about licking the competition!

Anteater

TOTAL SOLAR ECLIPSES AREN'T RARE.

A total solar eclipse happens somewhere on **Earth** about every **18 MONTHS.**

That's about **52 TIMES** in an **average American's life.**

But **in your town,** a total solar eclipse is visible only about once every **400 YEARS.**

And in **650 MILLION** years, a total solar eclipse will be very rare; it won't be visible at all because the **moon is slowly drifting away from Earth.**

More moon, more **HOWLING!**

What's the HURRY?

SLOTHS ARE

SLOW.

SLOTHS MOVE **SIX** TO **EIGHT FEET** (1.8 TO 2.4 M) PER MINUTE— **SLOWER THAN SOME SEA STARS.**

THEY **MOVE SO INFREQUENTLY** THAT **ALGAE GROW** ON THEIR FURRY COATS.

THEY EVEN **DIGEST SLOWLY;** THEY LEAVE THE TREE CANOPY ONLY ONCE A WEEK TO **POOP!**

Who you calling SLOWPOKE?

YOUR SKELETON IS EERILY COMPLEX.

Humans are **BORN** with around **300 BONES**. But **ADULTS** have only **206**.

The bones in your **HANDS** and **WRIST** make up **ONE QUARTER** of all the bones in your body.

The **ONLY BONE** in your body not directly **CONNECTED** to another is at the **BASE** of your **TONGUE**.

Every **SEVEN YEARS**, your body has formed a completely **NEW SKELETON**.

SOME ANIMALS HAVE EXTREME ADAPTATIONS.

THE AXOLOTL, a Mexican salamander, can **regenerate pieces** of its brain and heart.

All heart, EXTRA BRAINS!

To scare away approaching predators, **EURASIAN ROLLER NESTLINGS** **vomit** a smelly orange liquid.

In the winter, **two-thirds of an ALASKAN WOOD FROG** **freezes solid** and its heart stops beating.

SCORPIONS can go up to **a year without eating.**

COCKROACHES can **withstand forces** **900 TIMES** their body weight **without injury.**

177

STONE AGE
HUMANS WERE
ARTISTIC.

I'm ready for my CLOSE-UP!

Scientists discovered **40,000-YEAR-OLD FLUTES** made of bird bones and mammoth ivory in a European cave.

The world's **OLDEST HUMAN HAND STENCIL**—also 40,000 years old—was found in a cave in Indonesia.

CAVE PAINTINGS of lions, rhinos, horses, deer, and bison date back to about 30,000 years ago.

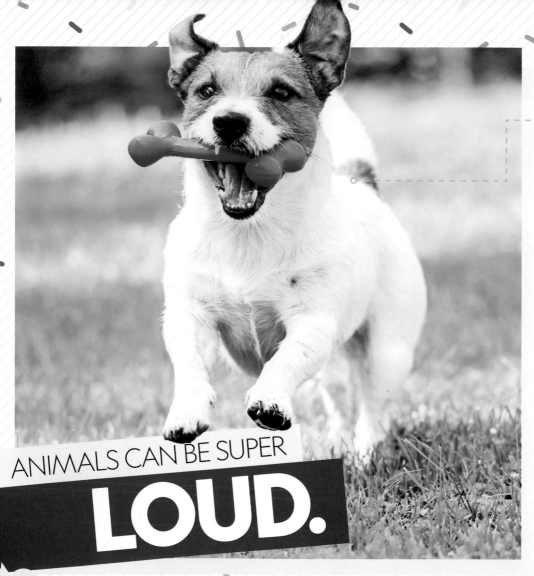

ANIMALS CAN BE SUPER

LOUD.

DOG SQUEAKY TOYS ARE AS LOUD AS **LAWN MOWERS.**

A **BLUE WHALE'S** CALL IS LOUDER THAN **A JET** AT **TAKEOFF.**

Time for an ENCORE!

BY RUBBING ITS **WINGS** TOGETHER, **A CRICKET** PRODUCES A SOUND AS LOUD AS A **ROCK CONCERT.**

ELEPHANTS MAKE **RUMBLING** SOUNDS THAT CAN BE HEARD BY OTHER ELEPHANTS UP TO **SIX MILES** (10 KM) AWAY.

THE SAHARA IS EXTREME.

Parts of the Sahara **receive less than one inch** (2.5 cm) of rain each year.

Nighttime temperatures in the Sahara are about the same as **summer temperatures** in the **Arctic.**

Even the **animals are extreme:** SuperCroc, a **crocodile-like** animal **as long as a bus,** roamed what is now the Sahara **110 million** years ago.

All ABOARD!

183

CAMELS:
TAKING THE HEAT

There's a reason camels earned the nickname "ships of the desert." For nearly 2,000 years, they have helped people move goods and supplies through the Saharan landscape, which can reach temperatures above 130°F (54°C). How do they do it? Camels can guzzle 30 gallons (114 L) of water at a time, then walk for 17 days without drinking another drop—or eating. That's a major advantage when traversing a land that receives as little as one inch (2.5 cm) of rain a year in some parts.

Camels have unique adaptations that are key to their success in withstanding the desert conditions and managing hard work. That hump on an Arabian camel's back isn't a holding tank for water; it stores up to 80 pounds (36 kg) of fat! When food is scarce, the fat breaks down into water and energy to keep the camel going. If a camel's hump droops, it means fat levels are low—but the hump will stand up again once the camel has eaten and rested. Other excellent desert adaptations: nostrils that close to keep the sand out, two rows of long eyelashes to protect their eyes from blowing sand, and supertough lips that can withstand thorny desert vegetation. And their thick toe pads were made for walking, allowing them to cruise through rocky terrain and sand at speeds of 10 miles an hour (16 km/h) for a steady 18 hours. Talk about all-terrain transportation!

TIME PASSES FASTER THE HIGHER UP YOU ARE.

A year on **MOUNT EVEREST** lasts **15 MICROSECONDS** longer than one at **SEA LEVEL.**

But even though they're **HIGH UP**, astronauts in space actually **AGE MORE SLOWLY** than people on Earth because they're moving **SO QUICKLY.**

An astronaut who spends **10 YEARS** on the International Space Station will be **0.1 SECOND YOUNGER** when she returns.

I'm young at **HEART!**

ATOMS ARE
TINY.

AN ATOM IS **ONE TEN-MILLIONTH OF A MILLIMETER** WIDE.

A **SINGLE HUMAN HAIR** IS APPROXIMATELY AS WIDE AS **500,000 ATOMS** STACKED ON TOP OF ONE ANOTHER.

SMALL but **powerful!**

99.9999999999996% OF AN ATOM IS **EMPTY SPACE.**

THE CENTER OF THE EARTH IS A LONG WAY DOWN.

You'd have to dig a hole **3,959 MILES** (6,371 km) **DEEP** to reach the center of the Earth.

If you could **jump in a tunnel** that went to the **center of the planet,** you would be

FREE-FALLING FOR 19 MINUTES.

The center of the Earth is so far down that the **pressure at its inner core** is more than

THREE MILLION TIMES

the **pressure at Earth's surface.**

WATER IS EVERYWHERE!

Almost **three-quarters** of **Earth's surface** is covered in water.

The **human brain** is **75 percent** water.

A **thunderhead cloud** can hold more than **2 billion pounds** (907,184,740 kg) of **water**.

NATURAL DISASTERS ARE
FURIOUS FORCES.

Erupting volcanoes can **throw rocks** at speeds up to **800 miles** an hour (1,287 km/h).

A **Category 5 hurricane** generates winds that can travel more than **200 miles** an hour (322 km/h).

A **tsunami** can move across the ocean at the same speed as a **Boeing 747.**

A **tropical cyclone** can release as much energy as **10,000 nuclear bombs.**

A magnitude **9 earthquake** releases about as much energy as **99,000,000 tons** (89,811,289 t) of TNT does.

It's all
RELATIVE!

HUMANS ARE CLOSELY RELATED TO THE
GREAT APES.

The **GENETIC DIFFERENCE** between **HUMANS** and **CHIMPANZEES** is **ABOUT 1%.**

That's only **10 TIMES** the genetic difference between **INDIVIDUAL HUMANS.**

And some SCIENTISTS believe that HUMANS and BONOBOS may be even MORE CLOSELY RELATED.

NEW YORK'S CENTRAL PARK
IS CHOCK-FULL OF

HISTORY.

IN THE EARLY **1800s**, THE AREA WHERE CENTRAL PARK NOW STANDS WAS A SETTLEMENT CALLED **SENECA VILLAGE.**

IT WAS **DESIGNED** WITH CURVED ROADS TO **DISCOURAGE HORSE AND CARRIAGE RACING.**

THE PARK'S **OLDEST MONUMENT** IS A 3,500-YEAR-OLD ANCIENT EGYPTIAN OBELISK CALLED **CLEOPATRA'S NEEDLE.**

I'm just **HORSING** around!

INDEX

Boldface indicates illustrations.

PHOTO CREDITS

ASP: Alamy Stock Photo; DT: Dreamstime; GI: Getty Images; SS: Shutterstock

Cover (UP RT), SSSCCC/SS; (candy letters), Henk Dawson; (LO RT), Erik Lam/SS; (LO LE), Kevkhiev Yury/DT; (pizza), bestv/SS; (ball), irin-k/SS; (UP LE), DM7/SS; spine, Erik Lam/SS; back cover (mouse), Rudmer Zwerver/SS; (lollipop), Volodymyr Krasyuk/SS; (LE), Ruth Black/SS; (CTR), Andrey Pavlov/DT; (RT), Photo by DEA/V. Pirozzi/De Agostini/GI

Interior 1 (mouse), Rudmer Zwerver/SS; 1 (lollipop), Volodymyr Krasyuk/SS; 1 (LO), Sergey_Peterman/GI; 2, tea maeklong/SS; 3 (candy letters), Henk Dawson; 4, Erik Lam/SS; 5 (CTR LE), Elenamiv/SS; 5 (LO LE), irin-k/SS; 5 (LO CTR), Ziva_K/GI; 5 (LO RT), robert_s/SS; 6 (Background), LUMIKK555/SS; 7 (LE), Photo by DEA/V. Pirozzi/De Agostini/GI; 7 (UP RT), Andrey Pavlov/DT; 7 (LO RT), Ruth Black/SS; 8 (Background), EFKS/SS; 8 (LO), Javier Brosch/SS; 9 (UP RT), Aaron Amat/SS; 9 (CTR LE), Irochka_T/GI; 9 (LO), bloodua/GI; 10, wundervisuals/GI; 11 (UP RT), matkub2499/SS; 11 (CTR RT), oksana2010/SS; 11 (LO LE), Sinisa Botas/SS; 12 (UP), barbaliss/SS; 12 (LO), tobkatrina/SS; 13 (CTR RT), Ermolaev Alexander/SS; 13 (LO), Flynt/DT; 13 (CTR LE), Ljupco Smokovski/SS; 14, otsphoto/SS; 15 (UP LE), Javier Brosch/SS; 15 (sticker), ducu59us/SS; 15 (CTR RT), SJ Allen/SS; 15 (LO), anyamuse/SS; 16-17, action sports/SS; 18, Eric Isselee/SS; 19, Innaastakhova/DT; 20, Plateresca/SS; 21 (CTR), Susan Schmitz/SS; 21 (LO CTR), Srijaroen/SS; 21 (LO LE), Garsya/SS; 22, IsuaneyeSS; 23, Mookyoung Jeong/SS; 24, David Fleetham/Nature Picture Library; 25 (UP LE), wong sze yuen/SS; 25 (CTR RT), Inara Prusakova/SS; 25 (LO), ASDF_MEDIA/SS; 26, Gallo Images - Heinrich van den Berg/GI; 26, NG Maps; 27, Anton Petrus/SS; 27 (RT), NG Maps; 28, NG Maps; 29 (mouse), Rudmer Zwerver/SS; 29 (lollipop), Volodymyr Krasyuk/SS; 31, Evan Kafka/GI; 31 (UP RT), Eric Isselee/SS; 32, Somrerk Witthayanant/SS; 33 (UP LE), EDU Vision/ASP; 33 (CTR RT), Melica/SS; 33 (LO LE), Jagodka/SS; 34, Images & Stories/ASP; 34 (LO), Lobroart/SS; 35 (UP RT), Yongyut Kumsri/SS; 35 (CTR LE), SVStudio/SS; 35 (LO RT), vitec/SS; 36-37, PRIMA/SS; 36 (CTR LE), Ermolaev Alexander/SS; 37 (CTR RT), Andrea Danti/SS; 37 (LO RT), NASA, ESA, G. Bacon (STScI); 38, f11photo/SS; 39 (CTR LE), koya979/SS; 39 (CTR RT), Ingram; 39 (LO),

rangizzz/SS; 40, guteksk7/SS; 41, FotoYakov/SS; 42 (UP RT), Sashkin/SS; 42 (LO LE), billdayone/SS; 43, David Aguilar; 43 (LO RT), Visual Generation/SS; 44, PongMoji/SS; 45 (UP RT), Yann hubert/SS; 45 (LO RT), Okawa Photo/SS; 45 (beetle), Solvin Zankl/Nature Picture Library; 45 (CTR), Kamonrat/SS; 45 (CTR LE), Chones/SS; 45 (UP CTR), Brandon Alms/SS; 46, Ewa Studio/SS; 47 (UP RT), Dionisvera/SS; 47 (LO RT), mayakovaSS; 47 (LO LE), Aleksey Troshin/SS; 47 (UP LE), Maks Narodenko/SS; 48, PaulPaladin/SS; 49 (trees), Kittichai/SS; 49 (people), Rawpixel.com/SS; 49 (CTR LE), Anton Balazh/SS; 49 (LO RT), robert_s/SS; 50, TheDogPhotographer/GI; 51 (UP LE), Celig/SS; 51 (UP RT), Andrey_Kuzmin/SS; 51 (LO), WilleeCole Photography/SS; 52, kapulya/GI; 53 (LE), by CaoWei/GI; 53 (RT), Greenery/SS; 55, KJimages/GI; 56, Cyhel/SS; 57 (UP RT), imageBROKER/SS; 57 (CTR LE), The Natural History Museum/ASP; 57 (LO RT), Yusran Abdul Rahman/SS; 58, Daria Medvedeva/SS; 59 (LE), Eric Isselee/SS; 59 (RT), Tracy Hebden/DT; 60, EDB Image Archive/ASP; 61 (UP LE), Photodisc; 61 (UP RT), Bryan Solomon/SS; 61 (LO), unpict/SS; 62, Johan Larson/SS; 63 (UP), Edward Haylan/SS; 63 (LO), Paul Nevin/GI; 64, Jan Pokorn/DT; 65 (UP), Dave Watts/ASP; 65 (LO), ANT Photo Library/Science Source; 66, Susan Schmitz/SS; 67 (LE), Roland Seitre/Minden Pictures; 67 (RT), Fairfax Media/Fairfax Media via GI; 68-69, Hidehiro Kigawa/GI; 70, Heritage Auctions, Dallas; 71 (LE), Brand X; 71 (RT), Peter Spirer/DT; 72, superjoseph/SS; 73 (UP), Steve Downer/Science Source; 73 (CTR RT), khlungcenter/SS; 73 (LO RT), Danté Fenolio/Science Source; 73 (LO LE), Howard Chew/ASP; 73 (CTR LE), Ted Kinsman/Science Source; 74-75, Press Association via AP Images; 76, harmpeti/SS; 77 (UP RT), MaraZe/SS; 77 (CTR RT), classpics/GI; 77 (LO LE), Maks Narodenko/SS; 77 (CTR LE), yuda chen/SS; 78 (UP RT), Anan Kaewkhammul/SS; 78 (CTR LE), Elena Rudyk/SS; 78 (LO LE), Talvi/SS; 79, Greg Amptman/SS; 80, TRphotos/SS; 81 (UP LE), StevenRussellSmithPhotos/SS; 81 (CTR RT), PeterVrabel/SS; 81 (LO LE), Mik122/GI; 82, oksana2010/SS; 83 (UP RT), Carol Tedesco/Florida Keys News Bureau via GI/GI; 83 (LO CTR), Red2000 Creative/SS; 83 (LO LE), alfernec/SS; 84-85, Henrik Sorensen/GI; 86 (UP), Carlos Yudica/SS; 86 (LO), filo/GI; 87, Library of Congress Prints and Photographs Division; 88, jamesteohart/SS; 89 (mouse), Rudmer Zwerver/SS;

CREDITS

Since 1888, the National Geographic Society has funded more than 12,000 research, exploration, and preservation projects around the world. The Society receives funds from National Geographic Partners, LLC, funded in part by your purchase. A portion of the proceeds from this book supports this vital work. To learn more, visit natgeo.com/info.

NATIONAL GEOGRAPHIC and Yellow Border Design are trademarks of the National Geographic Society, used under license.

For more information, visit nationalgeographic.com, call 1-800-647-5463, or write to the following address:

National Geographic Partners
1145 17th Street N.W.
Washington, D.C. 20036-4688 U.S.A.

Visit us online at nationalgeographic.com/books

For librarians and teachers: ngchildrensbooks.org

More for kids from National Geographic: natgeokids.com

National Geographic Kids magazine inspires children to explore their world with fun yet educational articles on animals, science, nature, and more. Using fresh storytelling and amazing photography, *Nat Geo Kids* shows kids ages 6 to 14 the fascinating truth about the world—and why they should care. kids.nationalgeographic.com/subscribe

For information about special discounts for bulk purchases, please contact National Geographic Books Special Sales: specialsales@natgeo.com

For rights or permissions inquiries, please contact National Geographic Books Subsidiary Rights: bookrights@natgeo.com

Designed by Amanda Larsen and Julide Dengel

Trade paperback ISBN: 978-1-4263-3437-5
Reinforced library binding ISBN: 978-1-4263- 3438-2

The publisher would like to thank Julie Beer, author; Chelsea Lin, author; Jen Agresta, project manager; Rebecca Baines, editorial director; Paige Towler, project editor; Michelle Tyler, project editor; Sarah J. Mock, senior photo editor; Joan Gossett, production editor; and Anne LeongSon and Gus Tello, design production assistants.

Printed in China
19/PPS/1

How SWEET!